Crown of Thorns

-A Marriage of Forms-

Bethany W. Pope

ONEIROS BOOKS

In association with
WWW.PARAPHILIAMAGAZINE.COM

First published in the world by ONEIROS

ISBN   9781291535570

The author would like to thank Agnes Cserhati, Tiffany Atkinson, David Morley, George Szirtes, Helen Ivory, Tim Cumming, Menna Elfyn, Maria McCarthy, and Bob Carling. She would like to acknowledge the *utang na loob* she owes to her family; Joy Pope, John-Nelson Pope, Virgie Castro, Day Pope, Katie Pope, Ruth Pope, Dan Pope, Shirley Rowe and her husband, Matthew David Clarke. She would like to thank the publishers of this book; Michael McAloran, and Dave Mitchell.

TABLE OF CONTENTS

Crown of Thorns

Joy: Thorns

Unplanned second daughter; blond, gap-toothed, squalling,
blood streaking from skinned hamburger chin and bitten tongue
to pool and smear on the Peter-Pan collar of the new
polyester dress your mother sewed for Easter.
Second daughter, always trouble but, your father
reminds you, a treasure deeply loved. He scooped you up
from the vast steps of the Masonic Temple
where white robed elders, in mimicry of church,
pinned a sign composed of calipers to Daddy's lapel.
Your mother sewed a suit for him, and for your Grampy,
though he was difficult to love. When he stalked by
your daddy gripped you closer, turned your stair-beaten face
into the harsh weft of his wool, reopening
your wounds, shrouding the new gold of his honor in your blood.

John: Blood

Your grandfather delivered you, slick from your mother,
hauled you from her cleft with hands as soft as his doctor's heart
was calloused. Afterwards, he sent her the bill, advised
her to wash the sheets in cold water, hurrying
or else the blood would set. He knew she had few others.
A life in poverty and dust for the youngest grandson
of the richest man in the county, who owned more mines
than could be counted on your new made fingers and toes.
You grew fast, caught ringworm, the pattern swirled in Celtic
circles across your plump cheek, and neck. Your voice burred
with mountain accent as you spoke fierce love to your dogs
and the groundhog you kept for a pet until it bit
your palm down to the white bone and your father took the head,
severed, in a box to Nashville where he tested the blood.

Joy: Thorns

Water and blood swirled between fingers, down the black drain,
soap stinging the tattered flesh of your girlish vagina.
Your gasping mother drew back the cloth and never flinched
her Celtic blood would not allow surrender
to emotions. Her body stiffened as far
as pregnancy let it. Beneath her breast your unborn
sister kicked against her borrowed bone-cage, never knowing
that she would die before her birth, her heart broke for you
the way your mother's never could. She laid her hard, strong hand
among your curls, the only comfort she knew,
calling for your father who looked, cursed his rage
and started drinking while she packed your lives in boxes.
He quit his job, loaded the car, left no addresses
for your Grampy to follow, though of course he tracked you down.

some pronoun confusion

5

John: Blood

Skin streaked clean again, fresh and new to the world
feeling reborn as the sea-water dried and the salt
tightened the flesh of your cheeks. Your mother basked
enjoying the heat, if not the sun, covered from socks
to cloche hat, preserving her complexion. Your father
brought you to Florida, following jobs; your rich cousins
visit you now. You've tasted the benefits of status;
no longer the fat, mocked, pitied child. You've grown
tall, made friends, learned to despise the jokes of bullies,
remaining unfavored at home. Your father sees
in you a man too much like himself, pre-marriage,
and bathes your smiling face in acid made of words
so that your features are losing their resemblance,
sluicing into a new form the sun enlightens.

Joy: Thorns

Growing flesh around the darkened hole death springs from,
the bark hardens around the hollow in the bole,
the secret place you love for no known reason.
Dressed in a chiton, playing the role of nymphic
servant to unseen Pan, you slide into the loamy darkness,
your wood-rot scented hide. Adolescent haunches
squat in soft soil. You have a shepherd's pipe you bought
with two week's allowance. Treated bamboo and garish
dyed bands, producing a sound your mind makes melodious.
The tree speaks with the borrowed breath of a wounded girl.
Saturday is for hiding, drawing strength from the earth.
Sundays still belong to Grampy, his evil, elderly
entitlement; right of patriarchy to penetrate
beyond the heart of innocence, which grows no armor-bark.

John: Blood

The natal place you knew but never understood
spreads like mold across the rocky mountain. Farmland
disguising mines, deep earth-places your grandfather bought
in exchange for delivering babies to blacks and poor whites
until he converted medicine to money
and practiced only on his violin. You come here now
to try for a blessing from the patriarch. Neither
doctor or lawyer, something else calls you, an echo
of dead Lutheran voices rising from closed mine-throats.
Can a child be both Samuel and Absalom;
two sons at once, one called, one chased, both grieved over?
You leave for university next week, to study
healing, not medicine, to silence the half-heard wailings
of the dead your ancestor buried prematurely.

Joy: Thorns

You never knew your spirit was twinned, body split
between a longing for purity you never
could feel and the urge to strut your span across the stage.
High-school was hard. You ironed your curls until they burnt,
Worked at McDonalds to pay your parent's rent.
Breasts grew at last, Grampy left you alone to plan your
Escape, fleet from your roots. You took secretarial courses
your father pushed (something to fall back on) and saved enough
to supplement your scholarship. Your torn spirit called
for theatre and dance, some skin to slide into, an ego
borrowed and strong, binding the wound he drove into your trunk.
You specialized in sluts and tragic heroines,
landed many paper parts, scraped the words into plates
you wore above your sores. They never healed, worsened, or closed.

John: Blood

Divided between *The Way of All Flesh* and the *Gospel
of John*, your shelf shows your spiritual split, an urge
for Fame and Calling, exasperated by a youthful
lust of a scented, soft, tangible variety.
Seminary burns your unblessed body up, you dream
of the tall blond girl whose tire you fixed, her back brace
not detracting from her studied poise as she explained
her latest accident. A summers worth of courtship
severed when she said, 'I could never be a minister's
wife.' A student actress. You flared your nostrils, raging,
while awake, driving your Ox-head into theology
though you are John, not Luke. She slithers up to you in sleep,
beautiful and scarred. In the night you are the wounded
healer, tearing pain from her, gaining sweetness yourself.

Joy: Thorns

You took your pleasures where you could, in bedrooms, on stages,
mixing codeine with wine-coolers at the after show
rap parties where you joined the groups of modern dancers
in Bacchic revelries, disguising the discomfort
of the cast you wore after the accident in June
which split your spinal column and totalled your car.
A drunken daughter of your home-town senator
plowed into you in the parking-lot of Publix
while you were parked, packing your nieces into car-seats.
Months of surgeries followed, your scripts rolled up
while you recovered at home and your parents plied you
with promises that if you stayed they would scrape the cat-shit
from the furniture and throw the broken bottles out.
Summer, you dated John. Another sweet, toothed trap, escaped.

John: Blood

Until the quiet voice you heard in dreams called out your name
you'd spent your days in contemplation, attempting
to sever the cord that bound your spirit's ecstasy
in God to the loamy human rot that spread in your heart
as though you were an oak that time had hollowed and yet
allowed to live. Ordained at last, you raised the cup
and blessed the bready body of Our Lord, surface whole
behind the pulpit if nowhere else on earth.
When Joy called, the girl who gnawed her own leg free
from the trap her family laid, and mistook you for another-
she'd learned that every love was poison- you took up acting,
played the role, desired. Until her voice, drawn thin
by long-distance wires, reeled you back. You gave her
a diamond, flawed in the heart, a seam of coal in glitter.

Joy: Thorns

Hauling your inchoate mind from an agony of flames
you strained to push me from your body, unable
to arch a spine fused solid with metal, you begged
the doctor to slice me out. Like my ancestor
he desired money, not mercy, and so delayed
my birth, an action which cost you more than metal coin.
A cluster of traumatized nerves writhed, cells mutating
into arachnoiditis, disease like little spiders,
webs woven out of damaged nerve-ends, dying slowly,
a long-burn that left your fingers ashes, cold and curled,
numbness spreading after a long decline. You slid into
immobility, stage-strutting spent, your flesh hardened
like the drained carcass of a fly hung up in filaments
spending decades suspended, weeping, waiting for death.

John: Blood

A cool hand pressed against a sweat-crowned forehead,
all the comfort you can give your wife, beautiful
as she is in this fetid enchantment, your blessings cannot
sunder. She shudders in the bed you share, intellect
burning out of her, fevered ash the open windows
bear and scatter. This is the end of conversation;
all your talk of symbol naught. You will retain her body
to care for, the husk of a dancer. Two wounded
partners cannot waltz. You have children you must scatter
to winds that have her memory; you have her loss.
You have a service to lead every Sunday, swathed in black
that is not quite mourning. You have her lingering corpse
to clutch in the night. Small safety from drowning-
enough to live by. Hollow trunks float better than whole.

Joy: Thorns

A touch to calm you in the coming night, your nerves aflame,
your brain-cells burning. You do not know your husband
by his hands, and yet he sooths, quiets your spirit.
Your children are memories; going, fading, gone.
Your wedding is a picture somewhere, shrouded in dust.
Pain is your inheritance from Eve, your life-long pithing
until you are a hollow reed for God to sing through,
your fevered mutters oracular, nearly speaking, words
John bends and heeds to- a still, small voice he never
spreads. This death music is entirely for him;
your valor for the world. Your raped father chose his death:
you've endured. Though you are flesh, mud scraped over bones
you still live. Your husband smiles, wipes foam from your lips.
There's hope, if not salvation, where life is found.

John: Blood

A body curved around your body: deliverance
from awareness for one night, at least. Thirty years
you've spent on this endurance race. You've learned to value
youth as nothing. Live the best, most truthful way you can,
it passes anyway, and is sweet in passing when
a lingering draught would gall your taste. You could not close
the weeping hole in her, though the heart you feed continues
beating. Love spent out on hope has some reward.
Lives of the Saints make for interesting reading;
They are compressed, all time reduced to the dramatic
Episodes- the means of death, the resurrection-
The long spans of silent waiting, boring day-to-day
Suffering cut out. And you are enduring it. A life
of faithfulness. Vacant, she turns; clutches your hand.

Twined: The Jewel in the Crown

Unplanned second daughter; blond, gap-toothed, squalling,
your grandfather delivered you, slick from your mother.
Water and blood swirled between fingers down the black drain,
skin streaked clean again, fresh and new to the world
growing flesh around the darkened hole death springs from,
the natal place you knew but never understood.
You never knew your spirit was twinned, body split.
Divided between the way of all flesh and the Gospel
You took your pleasures where you could, in bedrooms, on stages,
Until the quiet voice you heard in dreams called out your name
Hauling your inchoate mind from an agony of flames.
A cool hand pressed against a sweat-crowned forehead,
a touch to calm you in the coming night, your nerves aflame,
a body curved around your body: deliverance.

House of Masks

1.

My mother had a favourite; my brother, her
only son. It was natural. His blond hair never
matted, he had a small nose, he frequently cried,
lunging behind her thin legs when we had company
over for dinner. He slept shirtless with a sword and a
very tattered fedora that dropped down to his chin.
Every family has a delicate point of balance;
dangerous to tilt. I was not what a daughter should be,
head full of matted, tangled ideas, a tendency to
explode into temper, firing my cap guns
right into my mother's made up face, running my fingers,
sugarcane sticky, through her professional haircut. She
observed the style set by princess Diana.
No love is a conscious choice, we only plot expression.

2.

The uniform itched terribly, starch spreading neck-rash,
heat prickling armpits of clothes we bought instead of
eating. My parents arranged for a spell in a private
grade-school; a second rate place with third rate connections
instead of free education that brought no prestige.
Really, I approve of the impulse, though misdirected,
life is hard enough to rise above without poverty.
We were meant to ingratiate ourselves, climb
above a dinner of fish I drew from the river.
Silly me, I wanted to run. More interest in
hard, above-age reading. Dante stirred my wild blood.
An adventure in preadolescent paganism
required more freedom, an accidentally severed
dog-tail necklace, a talisman the posh disapproved of.

3.

I took to the trees, wild with an anxious hunger.
Life between worlds; the social church, my hammering heart.
I'd been expelled from three schools, the half posh private and a
very dubious experiment in Adventist
education. They kept kosher. I turned up and
devoured a reconstituted ham sandwich. The
fellowship fell apart soon after I refused an
obscure punishment prescribed for insisting God would not
rain wrath on me for reading fiction. He is the Author,
the writer of worlds. At home I disappointed,
required correction. My mother wore blue silk while she
educated my blond brother at the swaybacked table.
Every day they sat together, Madonna and Her
Son. I'd get off the bus; start scrubbing, cabinets, floor tiles.

4.

Filial love is never easy; it comes with a cost.
A responsible boy, anxiously striving to be a
man, who sees the judgment of the whole world
in the eerie blue eyes of his beautiful mother,
lives under a tremendous burden of worth.
Young man, work hard. Study, present the mask that love demands,
subdue every urge to be other than vision.
She will love you. She already loves you. You are no girl.
Envy the other; your wild, dark sister, who says you were
created as twins, one side of the other; the free, the
restricted, the loved, despised when she runs fleet through
evening trees, returning naked with hair dripping, skin
torn by saw-grass, ticks in the soft flesh of her thighs.
She gets the whipping you fear, while your heart is wound tighter.

5.

Now that she is gone, you breathe a little easier.
Order descends on the House of Masks. Uncontrollable
spirits have been expunged. You sit stiff at the table
contemplating Horus, wondering if real school actually
holds any benefit not found in self-guided study.
Outside, the futureless children expend their vague lives.
Other plans rule your life. You delineate verbs in dead
languages, the suit she picked out for you spreads rash on your
neck. You wonder how your sister is doing in the
orphanage, though your mother does not call it that. It is
her new home. Without her dark influence you can
order your thoughts, present your best face when the family
moves up another social circle. You will rise high,
enter the best colleges; easier with half a heart.

6.

Growing hungrier. Every day there is less self to
inventory. Makes matters easier. Less weight
requires less fuel to keep moving, but there is a balance.
Life cannot continue beyond certain parameters.
Girls grown thin keep the farm in motion, hefting hay bales,
reeling, high on no food, fuelled by knotted rope beatings.
Escape in memory made half-fantasy through longing;
When you shudder in your bed, sweating from fever dreams,
smile a little at the thought of your brother, musician
tired after hour spent repeating the sonata she picked,
Romance bought with stress and finger calluses. Her
only son, the classicist she made, pearl-toes to gold-curls.
No amount of suffering is worth that pressure. Better to
grow scanty, exhausted; remaining yourself.

7.

Sound of a stressed chord snapping, a mind warped from striving to
oblige. You could not keep it up forever, pretending
not to know yourself, pretending you really were that
living doll your mother loved you into. She never planned
on forcing anything, mistaking your need to please for
satisfaction with the life she plotted. You feared
that wavering in thought, word, deed, would lay you bare.
Instead you compressed desire into a hard, dense core
nestled far from the eyeholes of your new mask, deep where light
would not blaze your brain, the blue of flames at high heat.
Over the years the temperature rose. Coal compressed,
organized over time to diamond. You never thought Diamonds
could grind down again to less than coal, and that spark
which fed you, which you starved for her, could fade, whimpering.

Rabbit Trap

1.

Rabbit blood on my hands, cradling the body,
a truck-struck creature I caught crawling in the centre
between two lanes of upstate traffic. Eyes blazing pain,
blurry tatters of intestines trailing on tarmac.
I skew-parked on the soft shoulder, scooped the body
to my chest (blood against my visible rib bones) and
bent to lower the still-beating heart to the grass.
Listening to the hitching gasps, I missed the sound
of footsteps. An older German blond licked her lips,
observed, 'You must give it death, it's too far gone to
do any good for it.' I crossed myself, prayed
over the twitching bag of ticks, fur, bones, snapping the
neck as hard as I could to the left. And still,
my God, it was breathing. Weeping, its life burnt my hands.

2.

You pulled up beside her in the shade of the barn,
held out your arms. Though a stranger to her, you displayed
amazing compassion for the woman you work with who
needed release from her jacket of blood. All
day in the attic you endured her weeping as she
set the text the best she could and reminisced about her cat's
babies, who were skinned alive by a farmhand, slaughtered,
raped of life in a gesture he called love. You could not know
about the orphanage, how the death of that rabbit
inflicted it all on her again so that she saw
not the Gowrie text that she was editing but
something altogether different, a visual
pain-jolt carrying her back in feeling and brain to that
abhorrent place where life was nothing, and she stuck in it.

3.

Small, mewling things I hid behind the water-heater,
motherless as I was. I fed them stolen milk
snitched from the kitchen; took a screwdriver and
opened the shoddy lock that kept the food away from us.
Loud cries greeted me every timc I dipped in to see my
dear little babies; calico, black, marmalade,
almost old enough to wander. Their ears were
closed, their eyes were open. I stole as many
hours as I could between farm-work and my indoor chores,
enough at least to nourish us in this place of
starvation where my three-hundred pound house-mother
rationed everything but beatings and I spent more nights
entwined with rags and mops in the under-stairs closet than
ncar anything that could sustain my appetite for love.

4.

Eventually the small board-built shed proved too constraining.
What young, hormonal thing could be satisfied by
enclosures? Their waste built up in corner-piles,
drawing flies, and I grew careless with the door.
Babies, unsupervised, clamoured for sunlight,
yearning for the feel of grass springing up between their paws.
My day at the barn-forge pouring metal into moulds, a
young girl doing work a man would find tiring. After, I
found the yard scattered with the flayed bodies of kittens,
a battleground of pelt and ragged bone-flecks.
I saw a boy I knew standing in the throbbing centre,
Lifting a lawn-edger above his head, grinning slant and
Unaware of my terror-look. At last he turned, saw my
raging, felt my fists, felt his face as it broke.

5.

Everyone has three meetings with the Devil, and lives
three times in that role: Daryl was a hired farmer, just
old enough to buy his own drinks in the clap-trap
local bar. A fat face lead by brown paedophile moustache,
oversexed, hard up, he slid into the barn,
vetted the stalls, ensuring his human solitude. I
evaded him, hiding deep in the straw, my eyes
following him as he cornered the cow I'd bottle-raised,
loved from a calf, into the A-frame which held her still.
Animal abuse in every sense, a determined
Rapist cleaving the bound buttocks of the cow.
Even a broken, starving girl could foster the strength to
Attack, scratching the naked, pimpled back with ragged
Nails until he battered my body into the mud.

6.

Deliveries are difficult work for unfed girls;
babies that weigh as much as adolescents are not
lifted easily. You guided the wide brown head through
a tight red maze and out, joyous as a champagne cork,
zealous for escape from the mother that nurtured it.
Eventually your body breaks to labour, gains
A strength your small size belies. Shorn-headed girl, a
baby yourself and new to the orphanage, sees
opportunity in the jobs the boy deride.
Utterly natural to a girl with blackened eyes
than finding some creature to comfort her, even if you
must draw it into the world with your own thin arms?
Youth has a way of surviving great trials, of
heaving through the blood-wreck, starving, desperate for life.

7.

Endure, little girl, what you cannot salvage from life.
A night, a year, spent with elevated heart-rate, with
rape, trailing your torn genitals about with you
the way a truck-struck rabbit would crawl across tarmac
lugging its intestines behind in the dust. A girl
isolated from family, in the hands of a monster,
feels the same terror as a creature dying in the road
enduring the touch of the hands that will kill it,
enduring the stench of the breath that beats against its
neck; the fear and foreknowledge of a sudden snapped spine.
Dear child, be content with your breathing, draw an
invisible sheath around your exposed nerves.
No merciful, slaughtering hand will descend to save you.
Gather your strength; your turn with the knife will finally come.

Bloodlines
An Emperors Crown

Crown 1: The Outer Darkness
1.

Blood defines the course of lives, breaking boundaries,
Every action, every choice is weighed by genes, slanted
This way and that in ways we refuse to acknowledge. The
History of family sets the future in its tread,
Although we are not without some say, some voice, our
Names secure the base we brace against, our foothold, that
Year-round, we face the world from. My roots spring from the
Wet Newfoundland coast and the coal-littered caverns of
A mountain-top farm in old Kentucky. My father
Slid into poverty from the womb of a defunct
Blue-eyed debutant. His father was something else, much
Older, an ancient native line; a mix of blood and
Rash bolshiness, a seeming-self-determined obstinacy,
Never relenting. The choices he made stuck, setting our course.

2.

Letting the drops from human rivers find their course outside
A world unfriendly to new creatures, my mother rocked me
Underneath a borrowed roof, a manse-house in the country.
Getting me born proved difficult to a woman whose spine,
Hardened by steel-lengths implanted by a surgeon, was
Inflexible. I was removed, torn like Macduff from a
Night-hole cut across her delicate belly. My mother
Gave herself a break from modelling, a pause from the
High-octane life of the professional strut. No
Ignorant minister's wife, she'd held her own from
Georgia's best agencies to the frazzled coke parties
High in the penthouses of the richest designers found
In New York. Her snapped spine had failed her, diminished her
Necessary trade, her commodity body, my home.

3.

Old corridors find their end in death for loners.
An old woman died alone in her own basement. A
Kind old thing, by all accounts, my father found her
Sprawled out among shelves that could have served in any
War-time library, stocked with brine bottles instead of books.
An army of jarred, pickled foetuses, her lost boys,
The corpses she salvaged from the hospital's clean fires.
Her head was resting on a pile of birth certificates,
Edna scratched on the line for 'mother'. The lady
Died a virgin. My father buried her in a grave, her
Loves arrayed like canopic jars at her feet, against her
Open arms. A line at end in antiseptic
Soil, as clean as anything, ground from which no tough or
Tender shoot would spring. Dad prayed for me, waiting at home.

4.

One girl left alone, encapsulated by stone walls, finds
Love where she can. Separated from family, she
Draws her knees beneath her jaws and wrenches another
Hiccoughing cry out into the dark. Twelve years old and
Interred in an orphanage, the girl steels her body to
Lie for hours in the damp hall closet. Her housemother may
Leave her there for hours, may feed her, or not, she
Cannot reconcile this life with the one she remembers.
Out there in the world her mother lies in wretchedness,
Unbroken by her shattered spine, though aching, and
Not capable of caring for her children. So this girl,
The eldest daughter that she pampered in the borrowed manse
Resides in danger. The mountainous monster who rules
Years will unlatch the door again, and beat her.

5.

Delight in the small things. A ray of light penetrating
Every crack in the wood walls of the barn allows
Entry to moonlight. Dream again of the times you
Ploughed into the river like a tern, the deep water
Incredibly cold on your nine-year-old skin. You were
Never a bad child, though a little unruly, left
To your own devices while your family climbed as
High as they could up the social ladder, all the while
Entirely unburdened by money. You loved the
Stench of brackish water, the feel of muck, fish droppings,
Odious but good, up to your thighs as you sank
Under the waves. Remember that now as you squat in
The barn amidst the heat and stench of cattle, your
Heart pounding, afraid, of what shadow will grow solid next.

6.

Blue-grey shadows. Dust hanging barn where cattle die
Engorged with milk, force fattened veal staked to the wall. It is
An entrance to the underworld where a young girl
Undertakes the role of both slave and queen. She is
The one who holds the shears, slicing the supple skin of
Incipient calf scrotums, snipping the vas and
Filling the bucket at her feet with gleaming testicles
Until the mouth of it brims with peeled lychee-fruit.
Loathing herself, she snips and ties, sealing the broken,
Leaking veins with black tar. She would flee if she could.
A taste for cruelty, a cool, clear distance, would save her
Now. She has no carapace, no hardened skin to give her
Distance from blood. She kisses their foreheads. Leaves them
Swaying on their wobbling legs, to fatten on straw.

7.

In the granite-floor blood-puddles, moonlight glimmers
Not that the broken-jawed girl notices the glimmers.
Cracked-toothed, gasping, she draws herself up from the
Reddened floor, crying incoherently for her injured,
Escape-artist mother. That broken dancer could
Dodge anything, even a shovel sent hurtling by an
Irritated half-man interrupted in rape. She
Bellows like a knife-struck calf, pierced to the quick,
Leaking its life out into the bowl, collected for the
Exquisite sausages that she will never taste. The girl
Flounders in air, bones-sparking. She sees her parents,
Each gazing into the eyes of the other, their eyes
Acquiring that deep love-look, the blinding veil that
Reduces everything, even children, to dust in air.

8.

Necessary to life, some kind of sustenance,
Everything looks edible. Dandelion leaves,
A salad of wild garlic bulbs, handful of sorghum
Relished in secret, stolen from the barn. And that
Leaves out the other kind of feeding. The books she
Yanked from the school library she was banned from
Entering, stories smuggled out in the slit lining of her
Very tattered patchwork jacket, plucked from donation box.
Every inmate does what they must. Some break locks, some
Rely on chain smoking to satisfy their hunger, or
Yield to the irrational rage that washes
Over bodies left hungry too long. This girl has
Never given into violence to quell that hunger, yet.
Every body has a balance point, an end to struggle.

9.

Devalued for now, a treasure hidden, buried in earth,
Every man-creature capable of contempt spat it out,
Veiling her in a mist foul and liquid like the spray that
Evacuates from the bottom of a cow gone off feed.
Little starving girl, starving in every sense; in her
Oppressed body, her grasping imagination, craving,
Perspicacious, her unfed appetite for love.
Eventually she found solace in the beasts, the
Dear faun-like cattle, the kittens birthed behind the
Water-heater. The rabid bat found clinging to granite
Eventually died but did not pass on its contagion.
Infection flourished nonetheless. Humanity
Revealed itself as an irredeemable state. She
Developed an uncomfortable urge to hide out-doors.

10.

She cups her hands against the place where breasts will grow,
Over her visible ribs, that empty place seemingly
Made to accept a wound. The shivs were constructed of
Every available thing. Hers was a bartered razor
Punched into the end of a blue toothbrush handle. Her
Enemy, her rapist, had a real knife stolen from the
Open kitchen. Her housemother handed her the key.
People do not realize that girls can rape. Media
Leaves this off the newsfeed. An unacknowledged truth, that
Everyone is capable of violence, even victims
Grow weary of remaining *that* self. This girl
Realized that she could make the violence stop. For her.
Even a jagged scar across the right pectoral
Would shrink with years. Look. See? It has nearly vanished.

11.

Loving the feel of skin spliced together, tissues bound
Over the irregular heart, I bottle-fed road-kill.
Near-death on arrival this Siamese rallied after
Every possible surgery. I helped rebuild her, made her
Stronger – in a sense. Fifteen years old and free from
Obligatory education, I worked for a vet,
Made the best of a situation not designed for
Escape into higher education. My father,
Obstinate, could not acknowledge the fault he showed
Relegating me to the care of the orphanage. I
Grew too traumatized for traditional schooling, though
Ready to heal at least some of the hurt. Vet-tech's
Eager assistant, I knitted, sutured, cleansed and
Wove patchwork creatures, flawed but alive, out of meat dust.

12.

Over the visible ribs, above the starved, thrumming heart,
Little bird who died because I could not feed it.
Dear little thing, entirely innocent, my mind
Wrinkled at the edges with fervent belief
In the end of the world. Apocalypse. I
Think I hoped for it. The redeeming death,
Heaven envisioned as freedom from memory
Or thought. I worked at my job, cleaning cages,
Underneath the surgical table. Antiseptic
Towels swathed on every surface while in my room my
Little love lay dying in a pile of her own green filth.
Odious death. I didn't want it for her. Surfaces
Very clean, all sparkling. My heart a suppurating hole.
Every hidden thing, revealed at the end of the world.

13.

Veiled by mortality, her eyes penetrate the mask
Early years drew over suffering. My mother
Rarely cried despite her spreading nerve-pain, those
Years spent in bed, not acting, writing, modelling, her
Foetid bed her home until her children changed the sheets.
Every family has a secret. Ours was our perfect mix,
Where hate met love. I loved and loathed her, her resilient
Exquisite face atop her mangled body which
Seemed an image of my heart. She hated my health, my
Carelessness with clothes, my monkey-face. In her eyes I
Aped a girl. My body which did nothing decorative, save
Perhaps my voice in recitation of hymns and
Even occasional permitted verse. She'd have gone to
Dionysus had she been capable. She went to rust.

14.

Every family creates, enjoys, forces on their members
Souls of their own collective creation. My parents
Carved mine out of cream-colored bone and bloody-leavings.
A spirit half-animal with vestigial seams of
Pentecostal Christianity. Do unto others
Entwined with nature red in tooth and claw. God
Dipped His finger in too, directing the story; genes flowed
Water-like, a hidden current that shaped the land
Above the aquifer, defined its contours, the curve,
Relegating arcs of cheeks and personality.
People believe that we are individual,
In terms of more than limited story, surfaces
Never reveal everything. Truth is also found in
Growing bones, in brain-chemistry, printed on our platelets.

Crown 2: The Ancestors

1.

Father stalked in, filth-swathed, hungry. His hazel eyes
Enormous in his ravenous head. A day spent
Walking through a hostile town, run by his vindictive
Father-in-law, seeking work that wasn't there left him
Angry, farming a thirst that bourbon couldn't quench.
Married three years and sinking further into a tired,
Inchoate life whose only vivid spark was Ruth, his
Lovely little blue-eyed wife. The girl he loved, whose
Ice-eyed German father cost him everything. He
Explained to the shop-owners, the mine bosses,
Sheriff's office that the marriage he had was not
Actually miscegenation, and even if it were,
Really it should not matter. He needed work, not
Explanations. The boys in the dirt cried for feeding.

2.

Ablaze with something almost light, more spirit than man, though
Still caught inside a filthy body, the Bible-reading,
Loving drunkard looked out across a field he did not
Own and could not till. His boys were walking home from
Visiting his in-laws, fed for once, but brimming with
Inciting phrases planted there to cause his hands to sin.
Now that he was nearly thirty, and the boys old enough,
Growing wise enough to comprehend, they spoke in
A tone that was more than a little contemptuous, not
Suspecting that if he took the Old Doc up on his
Threat-promise, if he left Ruth there with the children,
He would make an easy thousand; his boys would be fed,
Insulated from harm, but the Word would not allow him.
So he sat there, suffering, waiting to see what washed back.

3.

Muddied over, his heart-beat visible beneath his shirt
Young John Nelson dragged his carcass from the earth.
Fainting on the slippery crest, the crescent opening he
Angled out of (the cave gaped behind him) he blinked,
Thought about the delving darkness, the painted walls
Heretofore unseen by men awake. Bear and bison,
Early gods, scrawled against the limestone and he
Returned from them clutching the skull of one of his own
Time-lost ancestors. The empty orbits of the eye,
Hollows where the spirit dwelled, stared up from brown bone.
Earlier draft of the boy he was, the long dried blood beat
Glorious through and from his own red marrow. This
Old, young, man smeared the filth from his forehead and flit
Down the hill to house, to farm, his inheritance clutched.

4.

I never knew you in your youth when life pulsed vibrant,
New, through the veins in your arms. They were patterned on the
Veins that fed blood to the warped heart of your father, evil
Old German with advanced ideas. You, unloved youngest
Kinder, took what you wanted (like he did) but you were
Ignited by love. He could see no profit in it.
No measurable gain in the hovel you chose,
Gross stewardship of the body he gave you. Three times
Pregnant, belly sunk in debasement to the man you chose,
Rising from an ambiguous lineage. A brood awash
In bright delusion, that youngest boy, alone in forests,
Enquiring of God… You are my grandmother, my
Strange blood is yours— in part. You were as ruthless as
The old man. You took what you wanted, no matter the cost.

5.

Lush river leaping through the centre of the forest
Over deer paths and fallen logs, my father ran with it,
Variable and swift as the current, carrying the
Echoing voice of God that beat in his ears like a pulse.
Dust you are and dust shall you be, the subtext of an
Unequivocally southern sermon. Thirteen years old,
Somewhat fat, you contemplate Ezekiel, testing
Belief in the capacity of life in dried bones.
Every prophet must start somewhere. You set your course here,
Sliding along the riverbed, muddied with filth which is
The purest beauty. Even now your body is hungry,
Begging for something more satisfying than food, an
Unsuspected need for the mystic, things you can touch.
There is beauty in the world. Your priesthood is in it.

6.

Incredible strength, as Hercules' son, you lifted the
New ceiling beam (it began as a hearth) for your brother's
Theatrical house. Fifty-five years old, the boy-priest
Exchanged ministry for psychology, but faith kept hold.
Rough, ragged, indestructible, God cankered your soul,
Riding you like a bloodied stallion from pulpit to brain.
Edges always fascinated you, the question of
Destruction, creative or not. You strain yourself now,
Reeling beneath the weight of a ton of aged oak.
Engaged with this your brain blares Sampson,
God's Judge, who failed and rose. You are no failure.
A man who gave the best of himself to churches, scooped to
Rind, totally hollowed, you found something new.
Darkness edged to dawn, leaving God, you found Him in brain-
                                        folds.

7.

Enormous beams above your head. The house you built
Not of wood, the house of the spirit is ageing around
The grey tufts on your head. You were a drinker once,
Of bourbon, whisky, you wandered home drunk to the
Marriage you made with the girl from Town, the youngest
Blue-eyed daughter of the owner of the mines. You've had
Enough of struggle. You gave it up. The drinking, the
Daughter you kept— or she kept you. The cost of
Love drove you all down to Florida. The need for any
Other job than the shit shifts you took up when Old Doc, in
Vengeance, threw you on the black-list and the town shut you out.
Eventually you found a vocation, rehoming the
Otherwise lost, the mentally incompetent. Never
Failing, or admitting failure. Treasure, unwanted, kept.

8.

Somehow from memories, a world escaped, emerges
Maliciously in dreams. The children you bore,
All grown up, are babies again and they are drowning.
Little creatures, rounded by puppy-fat, your
Love for them billowing, inflating your breasts to their
Old form. You bathed them in the river, you whose
Father hired servants to wash you in the claw-foot tub,
Famous for three counties over. In the bed your husband
Sets the sheets on (because of the loaded guns underneath)
His body is bony, elderly, cold. Curl into an
Otherwise uncomforting form, find comfort in it.
Outside of your skull the night lingers on. Within
The babies clutch your fingers, breathe out their soft
Sweet breath. You dream a cold time golden. How it does hurt.

9.

Here in this room you once held safe, a woman weeps.
Exquisite in her agony, her scarred body shifts
From one corner of her bed, writhing nearly to the
Edge. The morphine isn't helping. Her painted nails
Lift the skin from her legs in ragged strips. Blood
That glimmers darkly or soaks into sheets. Her beautiful
Head is crimped at the lips, eyes leaking. This woman is
Indestructible in her slow destruction. She does
Not notice the small distress of bleeding legs or gums,
Damaged nerves swallow the surface agony.
Enjoy the Joy without her mask. Your wife cast down, you
Refuse to abandon her. You will not relinquish her,
Even if she begs for it. She is your best thing,
Death cannot have beauty. You are willing to fight it out.

10.

Eager for death, the help you cannot give, nor want to;
Not noticing the way that your children are growing,
That your wild daughter has been suffering since she
Arrived back home. You are engulfed in physical fire,
Not spreading past your waist yet, but bad enough to
Get your nails bloody when you attempt to scratch the
Little blaze out. You are a mortal woman, mother,
Entirely forgivable. Sometimes even
Death would be better than suffering. Better for us.
Incredible as it sounds, your almost-orphaned girl
Needs you here, alive. She tells you otherwise. Shouts
Over, 'Why won't you die?' passing it off as a somehow
Understandable comment, pretending that she aimed her
Rebuke at your moth-eaten dog. You survived.

11.

Love binds you to its evil course, limited by intent.
Incredibly you mean only good. You are alive
Tonight, wheeling your walker, the bright yellow
Tennis balls on the front of the frame smudge the
Linoleum. The small dog in the basket barks,
Enquiring something only you understand. Your
Light blond hair is perfectly set, a crown across your
Ivory forehead. A tight curl bobs against a blue iris,
Veins throb in your ageing hands. Fifty five years old,
Enviably beautiful, entirely mad,
Suffering unseated reason at the last. Your
Open eyes are blank yet weeping. You whisper to the
Unflinching dog who tilts his foxy head in false
Reflection. I watch all this from the kitchen door.

12.

Desire to climb above the wreckage of a life ruled by
Insatiable need ran me ragged into earth.
Realizing that the vet's job was getting me nowhere,
That my unused life was passing fast, I hung up my bleach-
Yellowed lab-coat, washed the blood from my hands for the last
time,
Crossed the street to the high-school I had never entered and
Left my known world. I took the tests required for seeking
Admission, passed with moderately flying colours,
Wrote my factual essay (they mistook it for fiction),
Hauled myself via greyhound up the Florida coast
And farther, into Virginia. Full ride scholarship,
Not counting the books. I called home occasionally,
Did not say much to anyone. I marvelled at the
Seemingly limitless wealth of my roommate from Texas.

13.

Burning passion for God, mortal happiness is second,
Importance limited by natural bounds.
No pleasure can withstand a worry this constant, a
Divorce far more dire than one set in a court.
Intelligent men struggle with pain played out,
Non-negotiable, on the bodies of their loves.
God ordained and man confirmed your ministry on earth.
How you balanced the two opposing forces for so long
Is utterly beyond me. Father, Aba, you never
Made a move to forsake her, even as she forgot
Her husband in her pain. I saw you massage her for hours,
Erasing the scratch marks she made with your thumbs,
Rubbing so hard that your nails retreated, your heavy
Eyelids drooping, exhausted, from bearing her up.

14.

Yearning for completion is the first, the only thing
Each human really feels. John-Nelson reaches down,
Arranges his wife's blond hair delicately across her
Red pillow, remembering the way she moved those early
Nights. She would speed to his door in her forest-green Spider,
Incandescent lights skittering across smooth paint. His
Name on her plum lips, she bent, opened the door and he
Got in. Vivaldi on the 8-track, Four Seasons: Spring.
They fell onto the beach and danced in the sand-spray,
Open eyes stinging with salt-mist, she leaned in. Her
Slight weight pressed against his good polyester,
Open at the chest, the few scant hairs she fondled.
Incredible, now, that it ever happened. She shivers,
Laughs— a sound without meaning. He might be alone.

Crown 3: Alchemy

1

Ordinary lives are not for us. We are children,
Not so different from the others on earth.
Love is a great, destructive force; like oxygen.
Yearning to breathe, craving the fuel that rusts us down,
Little by little, until we are red ashes. Caught in
Oppressive webs of life, we grew hungry, my siblings,
Veritably starved, though not in our bodies,
Enclosed as we were by disease and delusion.
Can you imagine? Year after year we clung together,
A little less sure of our desires, with less strength.
Necessary balance, the right amount of nothing,
Could have saved us. If you had loved us less, spent less time
Unloading the weight of illness and false, perceived failure,
The gift you never would have laid on an enemy's head.

2.

'Under a high master, the work is difficult.
No sane man serves God. No safe harbour exists
That is not Himself, and even in his scented bosom,
Incredibly glorious, there is more than the shadow;
Each man faces death. A hero lives with it. Great
Teachers say that it is worth it, this sacrifice of all.
He made, will unmake us; death is the only calm.
Enough rough philosophy.' Father waves his right hand.
'Know that He is worth all suffering. Your mother
Never really got to live. Escaping her grandfather,
Overcoming her past left just enough energy
To keep her heart whole in illness. She never
Overcame the shock, the broken-wing splinter she gained
Running through fate. Sift. There is meaning in the pieces.'

3.

Reducing bodies to dust, the matter of graves,
Entropy disperses us when we're not looking.
Noticing the way her large breasts sag, the skin
Developing wet-tissue webs across the cleavage,
The broken beauty frets her rare lucidity away.
Here in a house that renders few distractions she
Engages the oval cherry-wood mirror in a
Struggle for a soothing truth it cannot relay.
Her eyes, the same cool Icelandic shade as ever, her hair
Arranged in a mushroom-cap about her elfin face.
Cupping those breasts which nourished two children, she
Knows that youth has fled her, untried and untasted. The
Life she wanted, and briefly had, ruptured as her matter.
Eternity is turning her to meat-dust.

4.

Jointed bones, rustily articulated, turn
Over in their bare, stripped sockets. Joy, the dancer,
Inclines her remnant spine above the bath and falls into
Numbing water. Her skin glows red, the scars white, vivid,
Insulted by the cold they cannot feel. They say that God
Needed to scoop a rib from the side of Adam, that
God could not form Eve without a base. The cut that
Ushered me out of her body joins like a delta to the long
S-curve of laddered white formed when Dr Hogshead
Tore out her bone and replaced it with metal. She
Observed that Adam's trade was better. A rib for a mate,
The spine for a daughter. After his painless surgery,
He got up and walked. She waits to recover. The water
Empties, warmed a little by her body. Her time runs out.

5.

Over in their sainted beds, you lie with them,
Daring your parents to wake and find their adult daughter
Inching between them. Your father smells of cheddar, an
Odour you've known since childhood. Mom smells of Jean Patou,
Unguent salvaged from her life 'before'. She named herself,
Secretly, for 'Joy' perfume. Your father clutches you,
Paternal in slumber. One arm about your shoulders, his
Armpit hair brushing your neck. He hasn't held you like this
Since you were a baby. Such a shame you had to steal it.
This is what you wanted, then, when you were shrieking,
Terrified, in that under-stairs closet. Your mother
Holds your hand, breathing deeply. She clutches it in dreams,
Assuming it's your fathers. You are awake, feeling them,
Trembling. They could wake in a second. Force you back out.

6.

Included in the struggle for something more than
Necessities, a higher urge buried beneath the
Clear, cold fear of loss. You hunger for her; your wife,
Lovely, deranged as Ophelia in the pool, is still
Entirely your own. The last church you had,
Meanly, accused you of beating her. The small
Enraged Bible-Class Napoléon wrote you shrill
Notes which he slid under our door. The thought of her in
Tears nearly undid you. When the calls started coming, the
Greasy, false-concern which seemed to swathe the receiver in
Redolent stench of carious teeth, the sour voices
Aroused a rage you could not aim at anything.
Virulent passion made impotent by love, you sat
Entirely still in your chair, staring at her picture.

7.

Necessary comfort cannot bear the weight of
Earthly suffering. I am the woman at the window,
Arranging my books. Every few minutes another shock
Rocks me. That iron shovel blade connecting again,
Long years after, with my aching jaw. My back teeth are
Yellowing, but the false front incisors are white and whole.
Every day I feel it again, the rape, the
Violence. A hard tide smacking into me, coating
Everything in red. My fingers smudge the pages. I'm not
Really reading, I'm reliving. It never seems to end;
Years of constant re-iteration. My black eyes
Open wide at any sound; the scrape of spades in sand, a
Neighbour's child crying, bovine mothers wailing for their
Escaped calves. I never used to be this broken.

8.

Encouraged desire. Your love for her, a misplaced
Notion. Your brother, a shadow of a man, does not
Dare to speak from any meaningful place. He
Understands that your mother has placed a mask above his
Real features. She does not see the tortured scholar,
Escaping to his room each night, after his shift
Slinging concrete to fortify a bridge, to read his Greek
Bible and worry over conjugation. You hardly
Ever think of him, the cursed, favoured child who grew into
The golden glowering man who never sins. She
Welcomes him into her bed, the land she rules, even now,
Even after he broke her heart with broken promises,
Explaining them with circumstances that, though true would
Never be believed if they advanced from your lips.

9.

Dream that bursts when eyelids open. An intentional
Escape from memories, mostly your own. You see
A scarred girl advancing, grinning, with a broken bottle,
The neck she used on you. You see a streak of metal, a
Handle of a shovel, advancing for your smile.
A darkened cave-mouth you must enter to claim the
Naked skull that sits upon the ashes of a pyre that
Dwindled down from flames while half your family
Attended church in Scotland. You start yourself awake,
Clutching your ratty stuffed hyena—chosen because
This species mothers well—gasping wide-eyed at the shadows.
Usually you have to breathe a second, get up,
Acclimate to darkness. Read some Heaney by torch-light,
Linger on the calming passages, until the light bleeds.

10.

Romance, an intentional life, laid out in some kind of
Exacting pattern—even if predetermined, the
Soul spelled out by blood. Such was your father and his father,
Souls constructed from this or that genetic pairing,
Unique, but bearing markers of the old. Your father wed
Ruth in the face of her family. Your grandfather,
Easily thirty, abducted a fourteen year old girl,
Claiming that he loved her. She ran his business for him,
Transforming a dirt-farm into an insurance empire.
Incredible, but true. There is a rashness in our blood,
Obstinately reckless, once set in a course,
Nothing can swerve us. This determination I have to
Mould myself into something better? I got it from
You. You found God in a skull, in a cave. I found Him too.

11.

Order. Never mind the world denies it, the pattern holds.
Nearly thirty years since my birth and I see an all-
Encompassing order in everything. Easy to
Say that chaos rules; more difficult to prove it.
A long time ago my grandfather made a choice for
Love. My father was born, and then me. We sprung from
Veritable tragedy. My grandfather turned to
Alcohol, my father to The Book, I found my way
To poetry, a form which cannot be accidental.
Incremental design by one mind, totally
Outside the visible world, focused and burning, can come
Near perfection. The author of my life selected a
Mighty objective. A snarled skein, an unstrung bow,
Yearning for an arrow, made right, untangled.

12.

Outside of modern ken, below the surface where
No contemporary current can direct you,
Lakes of unconscious beauty spread in myth pools, fed
Yearly by the memories of our blood. Great-grandfather
Purchased his wife— young enough to be his daughter, black eyed
Urchin, native miner. She birthed Daniel, who sired father.
Returning to my mother, the suffering semi-saint,
I know that she and her father were both raped by
The man who thrust him into his mother. Over
Years, through genetics, these stories sank into my bones.
I am a product of my parents, in figure and fact,
Self determined by Vocation, will and by my marrow.
My blood made the form, I must fit. Every sonnet
Yearns for love. It doesn't have to be romantic.

13.

The corridors run, binding us together
Out of glistening blue and red wires. I begin to
Understand the composition of my body,
Generated from matrices of history and flesh.
Here are my mother's breasts, they rise from my chest,
Retaining the form they had in her lost youth. My
Eyes are my fathers; they entered the stream through his
Fathers mother. Flesh and brain, spirit, soul, an internal,
Unending source that mingles past and future, feeding me.
Salvation from misery, the remnants of an
Aching jaw, is found in reviewing the struggle. My
Life, redeemed through recognition of its features in
The faces, the stories of the ancestors who
Owned my blood in the beginning. I am myself, and them.

14.

Strong, implacable God-courses, leading us home.
Early life in the womblike comfort of my family.
Love flowed between us for a while, until disease and
Levelling fear dismembered us. I was created,
Made from the rubble they reduced me to in my
Years as a false orphan. An unseen hand composed me of
Pure spirit and my blood. The hand was not my own.
Our lives are woven from flesh and wire, the twisted ladder
Of our DNA, and a well-wrought literary plot,
Revealing itself at the last page, and not to us.
Somehow we strut our spans across the stage of history,
Obtaining the treasure; meaning. Thirty years and I
Understand so little, but this truth has been confirmed.
Love is the river that runs through our blood. We run with it.

Blood Jewels

1

Blood defines the course of lives, breaking boundaries,
Letting the drops from human rivers find their course outside
Old corridors find their end in death for loners.
One girl left alone, encapsulated by stone walls, finds
Delight in the small things. A ray of light penetrating
Blue-grey shadows. Dust hanging barn where cattle die
In the granite-floor blood-puddles, moonlight glimmers,
Necessary to life, some kind of sustenance,
Devalued for now, a treasure hidden, buried in earth.
She cups her hands against the place where breasts will grow,
Loving the feel of skin spliced together, tissues bound
Over the visible ribs, above the starved, thrumming heart.
Veiled by mortality, her eyes penetrate the mask
Every family creates, enjoys, forces on their members.

2

Father stalked in, filth-swathed, hungry. His hazel eyes
Ablaze with something almost light, more spirit than man, though
Muddied over, his heart-beat visible beneath his shirt.
I never knew you in your youth when life pulsed vibrant
Lush river leaping through the centre of the forest.
Incredible strength, as Hercules' son, you lifted the
Enormous beams above your head. The house you built
Somehow from memories, a world escaped, emerges
Here in this room you once held safe. A woman weeps
Eager for death, the help you cannot give, nor want to.
Love binds you to its evil course, limited by intent
Desire to climb above the wreckage of a life ruled by
Burning passion for God. Mortal happiness is second,
Yearning for completion is the first, the only thing.

3

Ordinary lives are not for us. We are children
Under a high master. The work is difficult
Reducing bodies to dust, the matter of graves
Jointed bones, rustily articulated, turn
Over in their sainted beds. You lie with them
Included in the struggle for something more than
Necessary comfort. Cannot bear the weight of
Encouraged desire. Your love for her, a misplaced
Dream that bursts when eyelids open. An intentional
Romance, an intentional life, laid out in some kind of
Order. Never mind the world denies it, the pattern holds
Outside of modern ken, below the surface where
The corridors run binding us together
Strong, implacable God-courses, leading us home.

Bethany W Pope is an award winning author of the LBA, and a finalist for the Faulkner-Wisdom Awards. She was a runner up for the Cinnamon Press Novel Competition. She received her PhD from Aberystwyth University's Creative Writing program. Her first poetry collection, A Radiance was published by Cultured Llama Press last June. Her third collection The Ancient of Days will be released in 2014. Her fourth collection, Persephone in the Underworld has been accepted by Rufus Books and shall be released in 2016. Her first chapbook The Gospel of Flies has been accepted by Writing Knights Press and will be released in 2014

Check out our other titles here;